ENGLAND

A PICTURE BOOK TO REMEMBER HER BY

This royal throne of Kings, this scepter'd isle,
This earth of majesty, this seat of Mars,
This other Eden, demi-paradise,
This fortress built by Nature for herself,
Against infection and the hand of war,
This happy breed of men, this little world,
This precious stone set in the silver sea,
Which serves it in the office of a wall,
Or as a moat defensive to a house,
Against the envy of less happier lands,
This blessed plot, this earth, this realm, this England,

"Richard II" Act 2 Sc. 1 32 48
—Shakespeare—
A.D. 1564 – 1616

PRODUCED BY TED SMART
1st EDITION 1975
2nd EDITION 1976
3rd EDITION 1977

© COLOUR LIBRARY INTERNATIONAL LTD.
Printed by I.G. Domingo and bound by Eurobinder,
Barcelona (Spain)
Published by Crescent Books, a division of
Crown Publishers Inc.
All rights reserved.
ISBN 0 517 18110X
CRESCENT 1978

CRESCENT BOOKS

SCOTLAND

Berwick upon Tweed

Alnwick

Whitley Bay
Newcastle · Tynemouth
South Shields

Carlisle
Hexham
Northumbria
Alston Durham
Maryport Cockermouth Penrith
Barnard Castle Redcar
Whitehaven Keswick Appleby Saltburn by the Sea
English Lake Darlington Whitby
Grasmere District Richmond
Isle of Man Ambleside Helmsley Scarborough
Windermere Filey
Ramsey Kendal Ripon
Peel Laxey Millom Grange over Sands Yorkshire Bridlington
Port Erin Onchan Ulverston York Hornsea
Douglas Morecambe & Heysham Lancaster Harrogate Reverley Hull
Port St Mary Castletown Skipton Burnsall Withernsea
Fleetwood Keighley Ilkley
Thornton Cleveleys Preston Bradford Leeds Scunthorpe
Blackpool Blackburn Grimsby
Lytham St Annes M62 Cleethorpes
Southport Bolton Sheffield English Mablethorpe
Wallasey Manchester Glossop Chesterfield Lincoln Sutton-on-Sea
The North West Woodhall Spa Skegness
Birkenhead Buxton Bakewell Shires
Chester Matlock Newark on Trent Boston
Derby Ilkeston
Oswestry Nottingham Spalding
Shrewsbury Stafford Kings Lynn Great Yarmouth
Ashby-de-la-Zouch Norwich
Much Wenlock Lichfield Leicester Wisbech Lowestoft
Wolverhampton Nuneaton Peterborough East Anglia
Bridgnorth Sutton Coldfield Southwold
WALES Ludlow Birmingham Coventry Ely Bury St Edmunds Aldeburgh
Leominster Droitwich Kenilworth Rugby Cambridge Ipswich
Redditch Royal Leamington Spa Northampton
Heart of Worcester Warwick Saffron Walden Felixstowe
Hereford England Malvern Upton upon Severn Stratford upon Avon Bedford Colchester Harwich
Ross on Wye Banbury Braintree Frinton-on-
Tewkesbury Luton Welwyn Garden City Clacton-on-S
Cheltenham Oxford Aylesbury St Albans
Gloucester The Thames Abingdon High Wycombe Southend
Cirencester and Isle of Sheppey
Stroud Chilterns Maidenhead Greater Whitstable Herne Bay Marga
Malmesbury Windsor London Rochester Broad
Bristol Swindon Maidstone Faversham Rams
Combe Martin Clevedon Bath Marlborough Reading Egham Canterbury Sand
Lynton Minehead Devizes Newbury Dorking Dove
Porlock Weston Bradford on Avon Guildford Royal Tunbridge Wells Hythe Folkesto
Ilfracombe super Mare Burnham on Sea Wells Frome Haslemere
Woolacombe Watchet Williton Warminster Winchester South East England Rye
Westward Ho! Barnstaple Bridgwater Shepton Mallet Wilton Chichester Hastings
Dulverton Taunton Longport Salisbury Romsey Southampton Lewes Bexhill on Sea
Bideford Wellington Yeovil Worthing Brighton Eastbourne
Bude Great Torrington Ilminster Shaftesbury Littlehampton Newhaven Seaford
The West Country Tiverton Chard Sherborne Poole Portsmouth Bognor Regis
Okehampton Honiton Bridport Dorchester Christchurch Cowes
Tintagel Exeter Ottery St Mary Lyme Regis Weymouth Bournemouth Newport
Camelford Launceston Bovey Tracey Sidmouth Seaton Swanage Ryde
Padstow Polzeath Newton Exmouth Sandown
Tavistock Ashburton Abbot Budleigh Salterton Shanklin
Newquay Bodmin Buckfastleigh Dawlish Teignmouth Ventnor
St Austell Totnes Torbay
St Ives Truro Fowey Looe Dartmouth
Camborne Plymouth Kingsbridge
Helston Salcombe
Penzance Falmouth
Lands End

ISLES OF SCILLY
St Marys

Festival Hall and River Thames, London *(Above)*
On the banks of the wonderful 'Old Father Thames', the Festival
Hall was originally built in 1951 for the Festival of Britain. It
comprises several concert halls and smaller rooms for intimate
recitals. It has been expanded as part of the South Bank Development which includes the National Film Theatre. The modern
aspect of creamy white stone blends well with the traditional
London.

The Life Guards *(Opposite)*

River Thames and Tower Bridge, London *(Top Right)*
From the days of the Romans, the great waterway of the Thames has been the heart of London. Though many of the warehouses of the Victorian merchants are derelict today, modern apartments are springing up among the old wharves. Completed in 1894, Tower Bridge spans the gap between old and new and London firmly resists any attempts to transport it to America as a 'museum piece.

The Houses of Parliament and Big Ben, London

London by Night *(Bottom Right)*
The famous dome of St. Paul's Cathedral is floodlit in the night sky and stands out clearly as a masterpiece of the architect, Sir Christopher Wren. In the foreground is H.M.S. Discovery, the ship that Scott used for polar research and which is now a Royal Navy and Royal Marines recruiting vessel.

The Choir Stalls of Westminster Abbey *(Above)*
The Collegiate Church of St. Peter in Westminster, under its less formal title of Westminster Abbey, holds within its walls a wealth of history. When entering the Cathedral one cannot help pausing and gazing in awe at the richness of this building. The view here is of the choir stalls looking towards the highly-decorated organ loft and stained-glass windows of the West Entrance.

St. Paul's Cathedral, London (Below)

Designed by Sir Christopher Wren and built between 1675 and 1710 of Portland Stone at a cost of £1,000,000 — a considerable sum at that time — St. Paul's is the burial place of many famous men — Nelson, the Duke of Wellington and the painter, Turner to name but a few. In 1965 the State Funeral of Sir Winston Churchill was held here. The height of the building, including the cross, is 365 ft.

Tower of London (Overleaf)

The Tower as it now stands was built by William the Conqueror about 1078, and added to at various times later. It served as a fortress, Palace and prison, and has many tragic associations. The White Tower houses a splendid collection of armour. The Crown Jewels are housed in the Wakefield Tower.

Clovelly, North Devon *(Below and opposite)*
Clovelly described by Charles Kingsley as ''a straggling village
of irregularly-shaped lichen-covered cottages on so steep an
incline that the base of the one is on a level with the roof of its
neighbour''. The single street of steps descends 400 feet to the
pebbled beach and a tiny quay, no wheeled traffic is permitted,
cars being parked above the village.

Goring Lock, Oxfordshire *(Top Right)*

The picturesque little village of Goring lies on the River Thames not far north of Pangbourne in a vale of the Chilterns where the Icknield Way bridged the River on its long journey from East Anglia to the South West. In the belfry of the church, built in Norman style, is an ancient bell, cast in 1290.

Henley-on-Thames, Oxfordshire *(Bottom Right)*

A well-known town on the River Thames, Henley is, of course, most famous for its Regatta, held each year during the first week of July. Much of the architecture in the town is Georgian and some of it earlier. The Church is in the Gothic style with many interesting old stones.

Magdalen Tower and the Punters' Station, Oxford
(Below)

The old university town of Oxford is still dominated by the buildings and traditions that date from medieval times. On May morning a 17th century hymn is sung at the top of Magdalen Tower at sunrise and this is later followed by a free-for-all on the punts with much splashing and pushing-in.

Royal Shakespeare Theatre, Stratford-upon-Avon, Warwickshire *(Top Right)*

Beautifully situated on the River Avon, the Memorial Theatre, designed by Elizabeth Scott, was opened in 1932 and replaces the original theatre burned down in 1925. Festival performances of Shakespeare's plays are given here from April to October. The memorial also contains a library, picture gallery and museum. The town of Stratford is renowned, of course, as the birthplace of Shakespeare in 1564.

Welford-on-Avon, Warwickshire *(Below)*

The thatched and timbered cottages of Welford-on-Avon nestle among the flowers as if big cities had never been heard of. The village maypole with its unsophisticated stripes and the old lychgate by the churchyard complete the aura of rural tranquility and friendliness that appeals to even the most business-like heart.

Anne Hathaway's Cottage, Shottery, Warwickshire
(Bottom Right)

By taking the picturesque footpath across the fields from Stratford, one reaches the pretty village of Shottery. It was here in this charming half-timbered Elizabethan farmhouse that Anne Hathaway was born. Many interesting relics and original Hathaway furniture can be seen in the cottage.

The Botanical Gardens, Birmingham *(Below)*

An unexpected glimpse of the industrial and University city of Birmingham showing the Botanical Gardens which lie hard by the famous cricket ground at Edgbaston. The town itself has many interesting old buildings, among them the restored Church of St. Martin where members of the De Bermingham family are buried.

Lady Godiva Statue, Coventry (Above)
Famed in recent years for the wonderful new cathedral designed by Sir Basil Spence and opened by Her Majesty the Queen in 1962, Coventry has many historic associations. One of the most famous is the old tale of Lady Godiva, whose statue is pictured here. The unfortunate 'Peeping Tom' is also commemorated by an effigy overlooking Hertford Street.

The Bull Ring, Birmingham, Warwickshire (Above)
The recently developed Bull Ring site with its modern skyscrapers and bright neon signs contrasts vividly with the older areas of this University city. Of interest are the 17th Century Stratford House, recently restored and Aston House, completed in 1635, which is now a museum.

Houghton Mill, Huntingdonshire *(Right)*
Attractively situated on the River Ouse and a popular boating centre, the pretty old village of Houghton is noted for its water mill pictured here. The mill, property of the National Trust, has been immaculately preserved and is now leased to the Youth Hostels Association.

The Backs, Cambridge *(Top Left)*
These beautiful lawns and gardens, much frequented by students and open to the public during daylight hours, sweep down to the famous River Cam which is spanned by several magnificent bridges.

King's College, Cambridge *(Bottom Left)*
The city of Cambridge is of course famed for its University, founded in the thirteenth century, with Peterhouse the oldest college. King's College was founded by King Henry VI, in 1441-3. The building of the superb Chapel was commenced in 1446, and took nearly a century to complete. The stained glass windows are particularly outstanding in their beauty.

Duxford Mill, Cambridgeshire *(Below)*
Well-kept Duxford Mill with its beautiful surroundings is one of many mills sprinkled liberally on the rich flat lands of Cambridgeshire. They once provided a source of energy for this thriving agricultural region before steam and electricity were mastered. Though most of them are no longer used for their original function they are popular as residences.

Epping Forest, Essex *(Top Left)*
Epping Forest, with its 5,600 acres of beautiful, woodland scenery, is a quiet haven not twenty miles from the great metropolis of London. The Forest has belonged to the City of London since 1863. South of the town of Epping stands Waltham Abbey, dating from 1556, where King Harold, killed at the Battle of Hastings, is buried.

Finchingfield, Essex *(Below)*
One of the prettiest villages in Essex, not far from Thaxted, Finchingfield has many interesting houses and cottages. The church is also of note, being Norman in origin, of which the tower still remains. An old post-mill still stands in the village.

River Blackwater, near Stisted, Essex *(Bottom Left)*
The pretty river Blackwater rises near the village of Seward's End and then meanders through the Essex countryside to Maldon, where it opens out into a wide estuary. On its journey, it passes the silk-manufacturing town of Braintree and the lace-making village of Coggeshall.

Willy Lott's Cottage, Flatford Mill, Suffolk *(Below)*
Willy Lott's Cottage is best known for its appearance in John Constable's famous painting . . . The Hay Wain. Flatford Mill lies near the estuary of the River Stour and it is in this area that one can find many of the typically English landscapes favoured by the artist.

(Opposite) a master craftsman at work thatching the roof of a house in Suffolk.

Tombland Alley, Norwich, Norfolk *(Below)*
Norwich is a city of great history. Once a centre of the wool trade, it has many venerable houses and over thirty old Parish Churches. It was the home of the "Norwich School" of artists and Lord Nelson went to the Grammar School just off this quiet corner at Tombland Alley.

The Norfolk Broads, Norfolk *(Top Right)*
Bounded by the towns of Lowestoft, Sea Palling and Norwich, the area known as the Broads is traversed by over 200 miles of inland waterways. The beautiful, green countryside is very low and flat and the stately windmills are a familiar feature. It is a popular holiday centre for boating enthusiasts from all over Britain.

Horning Ferry, Norfolk *(Opposite)*
Horning lies on the River Bure and is a popular Broads holiday centre. The picturesque little 'pub' in the picture is one of many offering their hospitality to the growing numbers of holiday-makers who travel the charming rivers and broads each summer in brightly painted boats.

The Tulip Fields, Spalding, Lincolnshire *(Top Right)*

Spalding lies in the heart of the Fen District, an area formed by the gradual silting up of a large bay. The fertile soil is ideal for bulbs, and the town of Spalding is the centre of the English bulb industry. From April to May, the fields are a blaze of colour when the daffodils and tulips are in bloom.

Matlock Bath, Derbyshire *(Left)*

Matlock Bath stands on the banks of the River Derwent at the foot of the magnificent Derbyshire Peaks. A spa town, it has medicinal springs and baths. To the north is Matlock, at the foot of the picturesque Darley Dale. Dominated by the towering Heights of Abraham, this is an ideal centre for touring the Peaks and Dales.

Lincoln Cathedral *(Bottom Right)*

The magnificent cathedral dates from the Eleventh Century. Its three elegant towers are of particular interest. In the magnificent Central Tower hangs 'Great Tom of Lincoln', a bell weighing $5\frac{1}{2}$ tons. The best of the four copies of the Magna Carta is found here and the building contains many fine examples of wood carving. Within the beautiful Angel Choir the famous 'Lincoln Imp' can be seen.

Trent Building, University of Nottingham *(Below)*

Founded in 1881, the University College moved from its original site to the Trent Building, University Park, in 1928. The park and the building were the gift of Sir Jesse Boot, the first Lord Trent. The University was granted its Charter in 1948 and now has over 5,000 full-time students. The latest development is a Medical School and Teaching Hospital on an adjacent site.

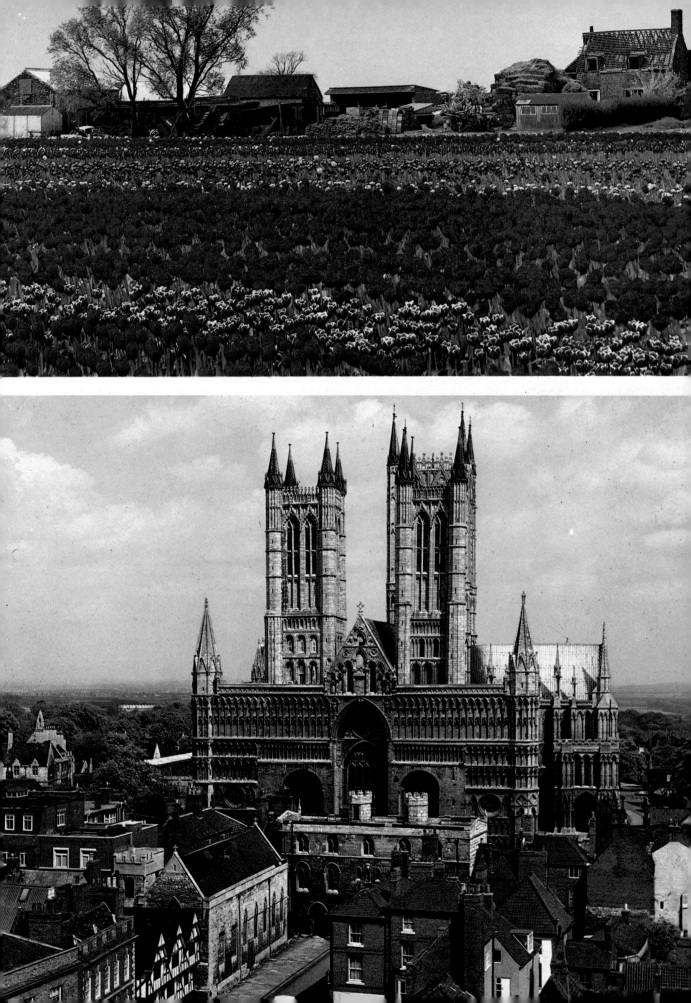

Muker, Yorkshire *(Top Left)*

Near the beautiful waterfall of Kisdon Force in the romantic Yorkshire Dales stands the picturesque village of Muker. In crossing the Dales the scenery changes from wild and lonely moors to the waterfalls of Wensleydale, the notable How Stean Gorge, near Lofthouse, and the potholes and caves of Ingleton.

Scarborough, Yorkshire *(Top Right)*

From the harbour the fishing boats put out to catch fish in the North Sea. The town is a popular holiday resort with a sandy bay to the north and south. The 12th Century "Three Mariners", originally a hostelry, is now an interesting museum and several other buildings in the town are of historic interest.

Robin Hood's Bay, Yorkshire *(Bottom Right)*

Robin Hood's Bay, a small fishing village a few miles southeast of Whitby, is dominated to the landward by the high Fylingdales Moor. The Bay, sandy at low tide, is backed by tall cliffs and affords excellent bathing. The magnificent cliff scenery is impressive, particularly to the south at Ravenscar, another small clifftop village with a little rocky beach.

Queen's Gardens, Hull *(Below)*

Famous port with extensive docks, Kingston-upon-Hull, as the town is officially known, is a centre of the fishing industry in Great Britain. It stands at the confluence of the Hull River with the great Humber and has associations with William Wilberforce, born here in 1759. A tall column bearing his statue overlooks the Queen's Gardens.

Bolton Abbey, Wharfedale, Yorkshire *(Top Right)*
Bolton Abbey stands on the River Wharfe some seven miles north east of Skipton. Dating from the 13th Century and now in ruins, the old nave forms part of the present Parish Church. The beautiful Wharfedale in the West Riding is part of the Yorkshire Dales National Park.

Fountains Abbey, Yorkshire *(Below)*
This great Cistercian Abbey was founded in the 12th century by Archbishop Thurston with twelve monks and it took three centuries to complete. Still well-preserved, it stands on the River Skell within Studley Park where a Norway spruce has grown to 156 feet. Nearby the church and house of Studley Royal and the beautiful Fountains Hall are well worth a visit.

Aysgarth Falls, Wensleydale, Yorkshire *(Bottom Right)*
Aysgarth Falls form part of the picturesque and tortuous River Ure as it winds its way down to join the Ouse. It flows through the pastoral beauty of Wensleydale, one of the less rugged dales of Yorkshire, especially famous for its excellent cheese.

Little Moreton Hall, Cheshire *(Below)*

Swans glide idly on the moat of the beautiful black and white gabled house that is Little Moreton Hall. Built between 1559 and 1590 with its carved corner posts and ornate windows it has scarcely been changed since then. The Gallery, with its original panelling, the heraldically-carved fireplaces and the great hall are all worthy of a visit.

Chester, Cheshire (Right)

The picturesque 'rows', with their shops raised above the street level, are unique. Some preserve fine crypts or cellars. There are many lovely old half-timbered houses, including 'God's Providence House', 'Bishop Lloyd's Palace', 'Leche House', and the 'Stanley Palace'. The 'Falcon', the 'King Edgar', and the 'Bear and Billet' are fine timbered Inns.

Chester Cathedral (Above)

Chester, the former Roman city of Deva, is of great historical interest. Much of the city walls remain, as do the attractive 'Rows' – old first floor shopping arcades. The beautiful cathedral pictured here is mainly Fourteenth Century and was once a Benedictine Abbey. It contains many fine examples of richly carved woodwork.

The Metropolitan Cathedral of Christ the King, Liverpool, Lancashire *(Below)*

The new Metropolitan Cathedral is a true wonder of modern architecture. Designed by Sir Frederick Gibberd, the outer wall is formed by sixteen small buildings, eight of which are chapels, separated by sheets of deep blue glass. The magnificent structure is crowned by a circle of stained glass windows so vast that a whole new technique in working the glass had to be developed.

Liverpool Docks, Lancashire *(Top Right)*

Liverpool is important for its university, fine cathedrals and art galleries, but most of all it is a port on the Mersey estuary with docks that extend for seven miles. The Royal Liver building in the distance looks on as the tugs manoeuvre the cargo ships that ply all over the world.

Liverpool Docks *(Opposite)*

This setting of Liverpool Docks belies its importance as a busy and essential link in the importing and exporting of goods. Situated on the Mersey estuary, the dockside frontage extends for seven miles. The University city has many interesting buildings as well as some fine Georgian houses, particularly in Rodney Street where Gladstone was born.

Blackpool, Lancashire *(Right and Below)*
One of the most popular holiday resorts in England, Blackpool has a rich variety of all-weather entertainments to offer the visitor. The Tower, the piers, the Pleasure Beach with its carnival atmosphere, golden sands . . . not forgetting the spectacular illuminations, all contribute to the happiness that Blackpool is noted for.

Derwent Water, Cumberland *(Top Right)*

One of the largest stretches of water in the Lake District, the lovely Derwent Water presents its early morning face reflecting the cool mauve of the heather-covered mountains. Coleridge and Shelley stayed at Keswick on the northern extremity of the lake and there are many fine viewpoints.

Lingmoor Fell and the Langdale Pikes, Westmorland
(Left)

Above the village of Langdale rise the famous, lofty Langdale Pikes and below lies the wild and desolate Stickle Tarn. The beautiful Lake District, well-known for climbing and magnificent scenery, stretches away on all sides — rolling hills and mountains interspersed with lakes and tarns.

Tarn Hows, near Coniston, Lake District, Lancashire
(Bottom Right)

Winter brings new contrasts and textures to the green mountains and blue waters of this delightful tarn, or small lake. Tarn Hows is a part of the wonderful Lake District where many writers found inspiration or relaxation; nearby Coniston is the birthplace of the writer and critic Ruskin and Lord Tennyson had a residence there

Wast Water, Wasdale, Cumberland *(Below)*

Beneath the peaks of Sca Fell and Great Gable the wild, lonely Wast Water lies in a deep valley. Fed by tributaries from the Black Sail and Sty Head Passes, the lake is drained from its southern extremity by the River Irt which joins the sea at Ravenglass. To the north is Wasdale Head, a popular climbing centre.

The Cathedral, Durham *(Below)*
One of the finest Norman buildings in England, Durham Cathedral stands above the River Wear on which the town is built. The tomb of the Venerable Bede is to be found here and on the north door is a 'sanctuary knocker' believed to have secured asylum for several hundred people during the Fifteenth and early Sixteenth Centuries. Parts of the Monastery buildings still remain.

Newcastle-upon-Tyne *(Top Right)*
Well-known port and industrial city, noted for the manufacture of armaments, ships and famous too for its coal, Newcastle was once the point where the Tyne was bridged by the Romans, known as Pons Aelii. Three magnificent bridges still span the River here, one dating from 1849.

New Civic Centre, Newcastle-upon-Tyne *(Opposite)*
Old and new stand side by side in this historic city on the famous River Tyne. There are many fine buildings of historic interest, notably the castle, the Thirteenth Century Black Gate and the Roman remains to be found in the University Quadrangle. Our picture shows the modern Civic Centre, completed in November, 1968 and opened by the King of Norway.

Lindisfarne Castle, Holy Island, Northumberland
(Below)

Lindisfarne or Holy Island can be reached, except at high tide, by crossing the sands on foot. Designated an area of outstanding natural beauty, the Island's old buildings are of great interest, notably the 16th Century Castle, recently restored. The Abbey, now in ruins, is of Norman origin and the Parish Church is also very old, dating from the 12th Century.

Dunstankburgh Castle, near Craster, Northumberland *(Above)*

Perched on the Northumberland coast, Dunstanburgh Castle presides over a stretch of sea and coast that has been officially declared an Area of Outstanding Natural Beauty. The ruins of this 16th century castle bear witness to the fortunes of war . . . it changed hands five times during the Wars of the Roses.

Brixham, Devon *(Top Left)*
A fishing harbour, Brixham is a popular resort for holiday makers who watch the fishing boats or walk along the narrow streets. On the quay there is a statue to commemorate William of Orange's landing in 1688 and a milestone marking the end of a former turnpike.

Polperro, Cornwall *(Below)*
Situated in a sheltered inlet between two headlands, Polperro is one of the most popular villages in Cornwall. Backed by a steep hill, the harbour is a most attractive feature and provides a haven for many colourful fishing vessels. It is overlooked by typical Cornish stone-built houses, the quaint old 'House on Props' being of particular interest.

Oddicombe Beach, Babbacombe, near Torquay, Devonshire *(Opposite Bottom Left)*
The busy and ever-popular resort of Torquay has many pretty suburbs, not the least of which is Oddicombe. The sands, sailing and cliff-top walks in this area are superb and Babbacombe Downs give excellent views of the coast line. For the convenience of summer visitors a cliff railway descends to Oddicombe and Babbacombe beaches.

Land's End, Cornwall *(Opposite Bottom Right)*
The surf thunders against the granite cliffs on the extreme south-westerly tip of England looking out to the Longships Lighthouse. Beyond, on a clear day, the Isles of Scilly can be seen and the coast is noted for its rugged beauty. By road, ''John O'Groats'' is just 873 miles away.

Corfe Castle, Dorset *(Left)*

Set in the lovely Purbeck Hills, this impressive ruined castle dominates the village of Corfe Castle. Dating from Norman times, it was the object of a famous siege during the Civil War. In 1646 it was reduced to its present condition by gunpowder. Many attractive and interesting old houses are to be found in the village itself.

Cockington Forge, Torquay, Devonshire *(Right)*

Cockington, a quaint little village about half a mile west of Torquay, attracts many visitors. It is famous for its thatched cottages and, of course, the old forge which is still in working order. Visitors may take a ride round the village in a gaily painted horse-drawn trap.

Plymouth, Devon *(Bottom Right)*

Plymouth, port and naval base, is, of course, most famous for its associations with Sir Francis Drake. Here on Plymouth Hoe he played bowls as the Spanish Armada drew nearer. It was from here too that the Pilgrim Fathers sailed in the Mayflower to America. Much of the town has been rebuilt since the war, as can be seen from the modern shopping centre above.

The Old Boathouse, Bantham, Devon *(Below)*

Bantham is one of many pretty villages on the inlets and creeks of the Devon coast. On the mouth of the Devon Avon, Bantham offers splendid cliff scenery for ramblers and sandy floors appear in the coves at low tide for sunbathers, but most places like this boathouse are best explored by boat.

Roman Baths, Bath, Somerset *(Right)*

At one time a city of high fashion visited by the aristocracy to "take the waters", Bath Spa is famous for its finely preserved Roman remains. The baths are fed by the only natural hot springs in Britain and, in the Pump Room, the waters believed to be particularly beneficial, can still be tasted. The central tower of the Abbey Church can be seen in the background.

The Winter Gardens, Weston-super-Mare, Somerset *(Top Left)*

On a sheltered bay in the Bristol Channel, Weston-super-Mare is a favourite seaside resort with good bathing, cinemas and theatres. The attractive Italian Winter Gardens with flowers in bloom all the year round are popular with summer and winter visitors.

Clifton Suspension Bridge, Bristol *(Bottom Left)*

The Clifton Suspension Bridge, designed by Brunel, spans the Avon Gorge some 245 ft. above the river. Beneath the Observatory on Clifton Down where a camera obscura is situated, is the entrance to the Giant's Cave. A passage leads downwards to a large cave in the side of the Gorge, an impressive viewpoint.

Pulteney Bridge, Bath, Somerset *(Below)*

Delightfully situated on the winding Somerset Avon, Bath was built by the Romans who made elaborate uses of the only natural hot springs in Britain. Pulteney Bridge, designed by Robert Adam, is flanked with shops and adds to the charm of a town that has always been noted for its elegance.

Chipping Campden, Gloucestershire *(Above)*
The mellow stone of the Cotswolds is enhanced by this display of spring blossom in the beautiful unspoiled country town of Chipping Campden. Once the capital of the Cotswold wool trade, the industry thrived here and from the proceeds many impressive manor houses were built. The Fifteenth Century 'wool' church has several fine old brasses and magnificent frontals—believed to be the oldest in the country.

Salisbury Cathedral, Wiltshire *(Top Right)*
The spire of Salisbury Cathedral, the highest in England, rises from the "water meadows" of the Avon with undiminishing impact from different view points. Begun in 1220, the cathedral has a dial-less clock dating from 1326 and the cathedral library contains one of the four copies of the Magna Carta.

The Severn Bridge, Gloucestershire *(Left)*
The elegant and magnificent Severn Bridge, Linking Aust and Beachley in Gloucestershire, also crosses the River Wye into Monmouth. It was opened in September 1966, several months ahead of schedule, and replaces the Aust car ferry which had carried many thousands of passengers during its 35 years of operation. One of the longest bridges in Europe with a central span of 3,240 ft. and side spans each of 1,000 ft., the road is carried some 120 ft. above high water.

Stonehenge, Wiltshire *(Bottom Right)*
These famous and fascinating prehistoric stone circles, of unknown origin and purpose, stand near the A344 — just west of Amesbury. Believed to have been brought from Pembrokeshire, Wales, the stones average a height of $13\frac{1}{2}$ ft. above ground and $4\frac{1}{2}$ ft. below, each stone being approximately 26 tons in weight. The whole site is surrounded by earthworks some 300 ft. in diameter.

The Seven Stars, Fullerton, Hampshire *(Top Right)*

What better way to idle away a summer's afternoon than watching a river from a quiet nook in the sun? Here at Fullerton, The Seven Stars provides a seat and refreshments while the weirs keep the clear waters of the River Test to a musical pace in the midst of the beautiful Hampshire countryside.

Swan Green, near Lyndhurst, Hampshire *(Left)*

Swan Green is the perfect setting for a friendly game of cricket. Situated near Lyndhurst it is an ideal starting point for trips into the attractive woodland of the New Forest. There are plenty of interesting trees and shrubs to see and a visit is made more enjoyable by the ever curious New Forest ponies.

Godshill, Isle of Wight *(Bottom Right)*

Godshill, a picturesque little village in the south of the Island, not far from Shanklin, is famous for its quaint old thatched cottages. In the village stands the 14th Century church with its square stone tower and old clock, noted for its chancel graves.

Southampton, Hampshire *(Below)*

Famous port from which the great liners set out across the Atlantic, Southampton has its origins deep in history. It was from the West Quay in 1620 that the Pilgrim Fathers set sail on the first lap of their long journey. From here too, in 1414, King Henry V and his army left for France on their way to Victory at the Battle of Agincourt.

Glyndebourne, Sussex *(Below)*
Concert goers picnic in the garden during intermission in style and formal attire.

Eastbourne, Sussex *(Top Right)*
A charming resort on the south coast, Eastbourne nestles beneath the South Downs. To the west the towering chalk cliffs of Beachy Head rise to a height of 575 ft. The town it self is pleasantly laid out with a wide promenade and beautiful gardens, a blaze of colour during the summer months.

The Royal Pavilion, Brighton, Sussex *(Bottom Right)*
The Royal Pavilion, begun in 1784, was rebuilt after 1817 in an Oriental style for the Prince of Wales (later George IV) who frequently resided here. Nearby are the ever-popular 'Lanes'. This is a small precinct of narrow alleys housing antique and bric-a-brac shops as well as modern boutiques.

Scotney Castle, near Lamberhurst, Kent *(Below)*
On an island in the middle of a lake, what could be more romantic than Scotney Castle? Though mostly ruined, it is all the more picturesque. The village of Lamberhurst is delightful with its old houses and not far off are the 13th century remains of Bayham Abbey. The adjacent mansion is the seat of the Marquess of Camden.

Canterbury Cathedral, Kent *(Above)*

The cathedral and rooftops of Canterbury seem to reflect the
timeless legends of the Black Prince's exploits, the tragedy of
Thomas á Becket and the Roman occupation of Durovernum.
By way of contrast, part of industrial history is also preserved
here in the form of the charming engine ''Invicta'', one of the
earliest locomotives.

Windsor Castle, Berkshire *(Below and Bottom Right)*

One of the first thrills for the visitor to England is a view of Windsor Castle. Not far from London, it is within easy reach for the tourist — and for the Royal Family whose standard is eagerly watched for. Originally built by William the Conqueror the castle is delightfully situated on the Thames and surrounded by beautiful parks.

St. George's Chapel, Windsor Castle *(Right)*

St. George's Chapel was commenced at the end of the Fifteenth Century by Edward IV as a chapel of the Order of the Garter. Its fine Perpendicular fan vaulting, completed in 1528, is of special note. On either side of the choir hang the insignia, swords, helmets and banners of the Knights of the Garter. It is the burial place of many kings, among them Edward IV, Henry VIII, his third bride Jane Seymour, and Charles I.

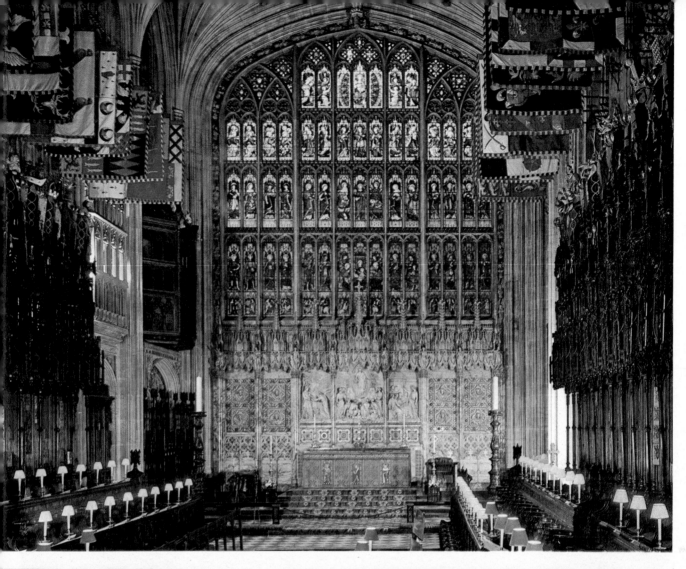

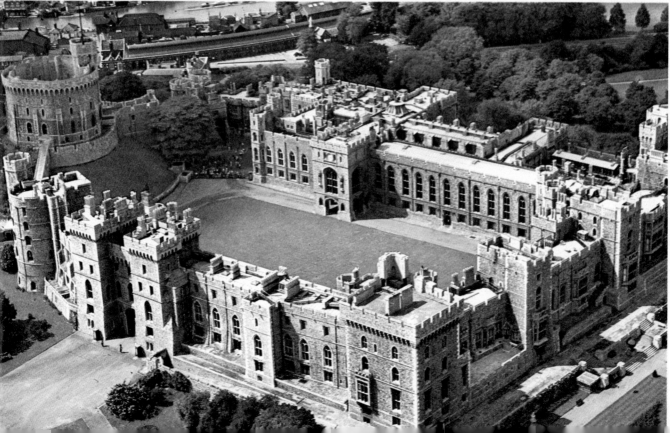

Hambleden Mill, Buckinghamshire *(Top Right)*
The old mill at Hambleden lies on the River Thames between
Marlow and Henley in the heart of the boating country at the
aptly-named Mill End. The village has a 17th century manor
house, a Georgian rectory, Roman remains in a small museum
and a fine church dating from 1633.

Polesden Lacey Estate, near Great Bookham, Surrey
(Above)
The great beech trees of the woodlands around Polesden Lacey
House make russet carpets for the feet of the rambler. King
George VI and Queen Elizabeth, when Duke and Duchess of
York, spent their honeymoon in this idyllic spot in 1923. The
house itself, bequeathed to the National Trust by the Hon. Mrs.
Ronald Greville, a noted Edwardian hostess, has a fine collection
of paintings, porcelain and furniture.

Kingston-upon-Thames, Surrey *(Bottom Right)*
Kingston-upon-Thames maintains a bustling individuality
amid the commuter suburbs of Greater London. Near the main
market, seen here, there is an apple market and a Monday cattle
market. A royal land, even before the Saxon kings were con-
secrated here at the coronation stone, Kingston has always been
a communal spot on the River Thames as proved by archaeo-
logical finds preserved in the museum.